Caring for Your Pet Dinosaur

Taking Care of Your DIPLODOCUS

Gail Terp

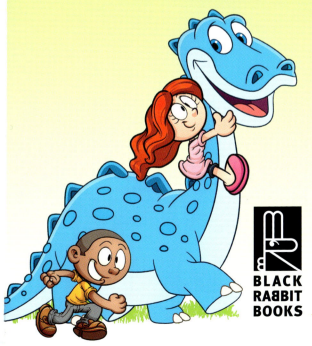

Hi Jinx is published by Black Rabbit Books
P.O. Box 227, Mankato, Minnesota, 56002.
www.blackrabbitbooks.com
Copyright © 2023 Black Rabbit Books

Gina Kammer & Marysa Storm, editors;
Michael Sellner, designer and photo researcher

All rights reserved. No part of this book may
be reproduced in any form without written
permission from the publisher.

Library of Congress Cataloging-in-Publication Data
is available at the Library of Congress.
ISBN 978-1-62310-6928 (library binding)
ISBN 978-1-62310-6980 (e-book)
ISBN 978-1-64466-5534 (paperback)

Image Credits

Alamy: BNP Design Studio, 12; MasPix, 14, 15; Shutterstock: 75ChuanStudios, 6, 7; Angeliki Vel, 1, 4, 6, 7; Artem Stepanov, 11; Big Boy, 1, 19; Christos Georghiou, 3, 16; dedMazay, 12; DenisKrivoy, 10, 11; Dualororua, Cover, 4, 8, 21, 23; ekler, 17; IreneArt, Cover, 3, 8, 21; Memo Angeles, 1, 3, 4, 6, 7, 11, 12, 14, 16, 19; MSSA, 7; Pasko Maksim, 4, 13, 23, 24; Pitju, 7, 21; Ron Dale, 5, 6, 13, 20; Teguh Mujiono, 20; Tueris, 16; Vectors bySkop, 4; Warpaint, 10, 11; wizdata1, 8; your, 15

CONTENTS

CHAPTER 1
Is a Diplodocus Right for You?...............5

CHAPTER 2
Understanding Your Diplodocus............6

CHAPTER 3
Caring for Your Diplodocus..................13

CHAPTER 4
Get in on the Hi Jinx..20

Other Resources...........22

Diplodocus is pronounced dih-PLOD-uh-kuhs.
We like to call it Dipi for short.

Chapter 1
Is a DIPLODOCUS Right for You?

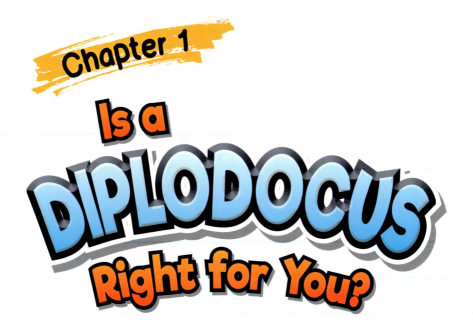

So you want a cool pet, huh? Something that will make everyone at school jealous? How about a Diplodocus? You could ride its huge 20-foot- (6-meter-) long neck to school. It'd become your best friend and help you get Frisbees off the roof. Having a pet Diplodocus can be tricky, though. A Diplodocus might not be right for you.

Chapter 2
Understanding Your DIPLODOCUS

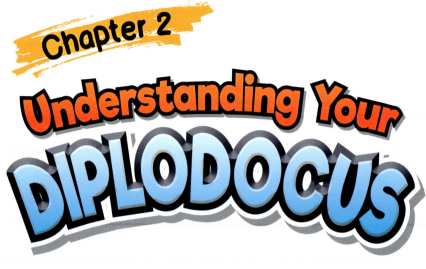

There are some things you should know before bringing your Diplodocus home. A Dipi is gentle, but it's easily startled. When startled, it starts swinging its tail. The tail is about 40 feet (12 m) long. And its end is like a whip. So watch out! Getting whipped by a Dipi tail would definitely hurt. A lot.

Some scientists think Diplodocus cracks its tail like a whip. This crack would be very loud. You'll want to cover your ears.

Big Dino, Small Brain

Dipi is a nice dinosaur. But it has a tiny brain. And there is no dino-school. Having a not-so-smart Diplodocus shouldn't be a problem, though. Just speak slowly and use simple words. A Dipi can learn easy **commands**. Teach it to sit, stay, and play dead.

A human brain weighs about 48 ounces (1,361 grams). A Diplodocus brain only weighs about 4 ounces (113 g). That's a little brain for such a big animal!

Gentle Giant

Dipi is huge. It'll be about 85 feet (26 m) long and 15 tons (14 metric tons) fully grown. But even though it's big, it's **softhearted**. Its feelings are easily hurt. Don't yell at it or it'll cry. Dipi tears are huge. If your Dipi cries, it might start a flood.

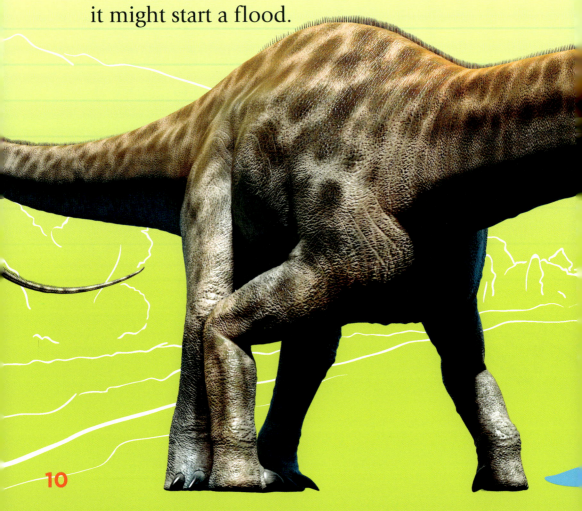

In the wild, Dipi lives in **herds**. So yours will want company. Spend plenty of time with it. But don't eat scrambled eggs near it. Dipi hatched from an egg. Eating eggs would hurt its feelings.

Chapter 3
Caring for Your DIPLODOCUS

Caring for a Dipi is a little different than caring for a cat or dog. Such a big pet needs a huge yard to move around in. But don't worry about building a barn for Dipi to sleep in. This dinosaur likes sleeping outside. It loves to watch the stars before falling asleep.

There's no need to exercise your pet either. A Dipi gets a good workout just by moving its huge body.

Big animals make a lot of poop. And scientists believe a Diplodocus' poop is mostly liquid. Better have rain boots ready!

Feeding

Since Dipi is so big, it needs A LOT to eat. Try to feed it at least 2 to 3 tons (2 to 3 metric tons) of leaves every day. Your Dipi will probably want to eat more than leaves, though. Consider growing a garden. A big garden provides lots of different plants. Carrots and peas make good choices. Diplodocus thinks peas are super yummy.

Grooming

Diplodocus likes to look fancy. After the pet's weekly hose down, carefully dry its feet. Then **apply** nail polish to its claws. The claws are long and the process will take some time. You might want to use a paintbrush. But please make the effort. Your Dipi will love it!

You won't need to brush your dinosaur's teeth. An adult Diplodocus grows new ones every month or so.

A Friend for Life

Owning a Diplodocus can be a challenge. You'll need lots of space and **patience**. But Diplodocus is kind and friendly. This lovely creature will live for about 80 years too. You two can be best friends for a long time.

Chapter 4
Get in on the HIJINX

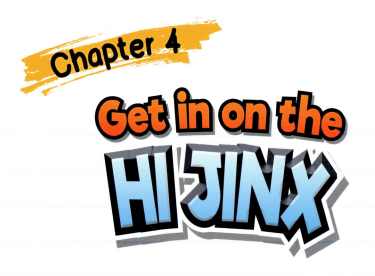

Diplodocus went **extinct** a long time ago. You can't keep one as a pet now, even if you have the space! Scientists still study them, though. They examine Diplodocus' **fossilized** bones and eggs. They think females kept their eggs in underground nests. These nests might have protected the eggs from **predators**. New discoveries like this are made each year. Maybe you'll make a big dino discovery someday.

Take It One Step More

1. Would you like to study dinosaurs when you grow up? Why or why not?

2. Plan a picnic with your Diplodocus. What foods would you bring?

3. Do you think such big animals would like living as pets? Why or why not?

GLOSSARY

apply (uh-PLI)—to lay or spread on

command (kuh-MAND)—an order given to a person or animal to do something

extinct (ek-STINGKT)—no longer existing

fossilized (FOS-uh-lahyzd)—having been preserved as rock

herd (HURD)—a group of animals

patience (PEY-shuhns)—the ability to remain calm when dealing with a difficult or annoying situation, task, or person

predator (PRED-uh-tuhr)—an animal that eats other animals

softhearted (SAWFT-HAHR-tid)—having feelings of kindness and sympathy for other people